MW00342814

ON NARCISSISM:
AN INTRODUCTION

BY

SIGMUND FREUD

Copyright © 2013 Read Books Ltd.
This book is copyright and may not be
reproduced or copied in any way without
the express permission of the publisher in writing

British Library Cataloguing-in-Publication Data
A catalogue record for this book is available from the
British Library

Contents

Sigmund Freud

Sigismund Schlomo Freud was born on 6th May 1856, in the Moravian town of Příbor, now part of the Czech Republic.

Sigmund was the eldest of eight children to Jewish Galician parents, Jacob and Amalia Freud. After Freud's father lost his business as a result of the Panic of 1857, the family were forced to move to Leipzig and then Vienna to avoid poverty. It was in Vienna that the nine-year-old Sigmund enrolled at the Leopoldstädter Kommunal-Realgymnasium before beginning his medical training at the University of Vienna in 1873, at the age of just 17. He studied a variety of subjects, including philosophy, physiology, and zoology, graduating with an MD in 1881.

The following year, Freud began his medical career in Theodor Meynert's psychiatric clinic at the Vienna General Hospital. He worked there until 1886 when he set up in private practice and began specialising in "nervous disorders". In the same year he married Merth Bernays, with whom he had 6 children between 1887 and 1895.

In the period between 1896 and 1901, Freud isolated himself from his colleagues and began work on developing the basics of his psychoanalytic theory. He published *The Interpretation of Dreams*, in 1899, to a lacklustre reception, but continued to produce works such as *The Psychopathology of Everyday Life* (1901) and *Three Essays on the Theory of Sexuality* (1905). He held a weekly meeting at his home known as the "Wednesday Psychological Society" which eventually developed into the Vienna Psycho-Analytic Society. His ideas gained momentum and by the end of the decade his methods were being used internationally by neurologists and psychiatrists.

Freud made a huge and lasting contribution to the field of psychology with many of his methods still being used in modern psychoanalysis. He inspired much discussion on the wealth of theories he produced and the reactions to his works began a century of great psychological investigation.

In 1930 Freud fled Vienna due to rise of Nazism and resided in England until his death from mouth cancer on 23rd September 1939.

ON NARCISSISM: AN INTRODUCTION (1914)

I

The term narcissism is derived from clinical description and was chosen by Paul Näcke in 1899 to denote the attitude of a person who treats his own body in the same way in which the body of a sexual object is ordinarily treated - who looks at it, that is to say, strokes it and fondles it till he obtains complete satisfaction through these activities. Developed to this degree, narcissism has the significance of a perversion that has absorbed the whole of the subject's sexual life, and it will consequently exhibit the characteristics which we expect to meet with in the study of all perversions.

Psycho-analytic observers were subsequently struck by the fact that individual features of the narcissistic attitude are found in many people who suffer from other disorders - for instance, as Sadger has pointed out, in homosexuals - and finally it seemed probable that an allocation of the libido such as deserved to be described as narcissism might be present far more extensively, and that it might claim a place in the regular course of human sexual development.[1] Difficulties in psycho-analytic work upon neurotics led to the same supposition, for it seemed as though this kind of narcissistic attitude in them constituted one of the limits to their susceptibility to influence. Narcissism in this sense would not be a perversion, but the libidinal complement to the egoism of the instinct of self-preservation, a measure of which may justifiably be attributed to every living creature.

¹ Otto Rank (1911*c*).

A pressing motive for occupying ourselves with the conception of a primary and normal narcissism arose when the attempt was made to subsume what we know of dementia praecox (Kraepelin) or schizophrenia (Bleuler) under the hypothesis of the libido theory. Patients of this kind, whom I have proposed to term paraphrenics, display two fundamental characteristics: megalomania and diversion of their interest from the external world - from people and things. In consequence of the latter change, they become inaccessible to the influence of psycho-analysis and cannot be cured by our efforts. But the paraphrenic's turning away from the external world needs to be more precisely characterized. A patient suffering from hysteria or obsessional neurosis has also, as far as his illness extends, given up his relation to reality. But analysis shows that he has by no means broken off his erotic relations to people and things. He still retains them in phantasy; i.e. he has, on the one hand, substituted for real objects imaginary ones from his memory, or has mixed the latter with the former; and on the other hand, he has renounced the initiation of motor activities for the attainment of his aims in connection with those objects. Only to this condition of the libido may we legitimately apply the term 'introversion' of the libido which is used by Jung indiscriminately. It is otherwise with the paraphrenic. He seems really to have withdrawn his libido from people and things in the external world, without replacing them by others in phantasy. When he *does* so replace them, the process seems to be a secondary one and to be part of an attempt at recovery, designed to lead the libido back to objects.[1]

The question arises: What happens to the libido which has been withdrawn from external objects in schizophrenia? The megalomania characteristic of these states points the way. This megalomania has no doubt come into being at the expense of object-libido. The libido that has been withdrawn from the external world has been directed to the ego and thus gives rise to an attitude which may be called narcissism. But the megalomania itself is no new creation; on the contrary, it is, as we know, a magnification and plainer manifestation of a condition which had already existed previously. This leads us to look upon the narcissism which arises through the drawing in of object-cathexes as a secondary one, superimposed upon a primary narcissism that is obscured by a number of different influences.

¹ In connection with this see my discussion of the 'end of the world' in the analysis of Senatspräsident Schreber; also Abraham, 1908.

Let me insist that I am not proposing here to explain or penetrate further into the problem of schizophrenia, but that I am merely putting together what has already been said elsewhere, in order to justify the introduction of the concept of narcissism.

This extension of the libido theory - in my opinion, a legitimate one - receives reinforcement from a third quarter, namely, from our observations and views on the mental life of children and primitive peoples. In the latter we find characteristics which, if they occurred singly, might be put down to megalomania: an over-estimation of the power of their wishes and mental acts, the 'omnipotence of thoughts', a belief in the thaumaturgic force of words, and a technique for dealing with the external world - 'magic' - which appears to be a logical application of these grandiose premisses.¹ In the children of to-day, whose development is much more obscure to us, we expect to find an exactly analogous attitude towards the external world.² Thus we form the idea of there being an original libidinal cathexis of the ego, from which some is later given off to objects, but which fundamentally persists and is related to the object-cathexes much as the body of an amoeba is related to the pseudopodia which it puts out. In our researches, taking, as they did, neurotic

6

symptoms for their starting-point, this part of the allocation of libido necessarily remained hidden from us at the outset. All that we noticed were the emanations of this libido - the object-cathexes, which can be sent out and drawn back again. We see also, broadly speaking, an antithesis between ego-libido and object-libido. The more of the one is employed, the more the other becomes depleted. The highest phase of development of which object-libido is capable is seen in the state of being in love, when the subject seems to give up his own personality in favour of an object-cathexis; while we have the opposite condition in the paranoic's phantasy (or self-perception) of the 'end of the world'.[3] Finally, as regards the differentiation of psychical energies, we are led to the conclusion that to begin with, during the state of narcissism, they exist together and that our analysis is too coarse to distinguish between them; not until there is object-cathexis is it possible to discriminate a sexual energy - the libido - from an energy of the ego-instincts.

[1] Cf. the passages in my *Totem and Taboo* (1912-13) which deal with this subject.

[2] Cf. Ferenczi (1913*a*).

[3] There are two mechanisms of this 'end of the world' idea: in the one case, the whole libidinal cathexis flows off to the loved object; in the other, it all flows back into the ego.

Before going any further I must touch on two questions which lead us to the heart of the difficulties of our subject.

In the first place, what is the relation of the narcissism of which we are now speaking to auto-erotism, which we have described as an early state of the libido? Secondly, if we grant the ego a primary cathexis of libido, why is there any necessity for further distinguishing a sexual libido from a non-sexual energy of the ego-instincts? Would not the postulation of a single kind of psychical energy save us all the difficulties of differentiating an energy of the ego-instincts from ego-libido, and ego-libido from object-libido?

As regards the first question, I may point out that we are bound to suppose that a unity comparable to the ego cannot exist in the individual from the start; the ego has to be developed. The auto-erotic instincts, however, are there from the very first; so there must be something added to auto-erotism - a new psychical action - in order to bring about narcissism.

To be asked to give a definite answer to the second question must occasion perceptible uneasiness in every psycho-analyst. One dislikes the thought of abandoning observation for barren theoretical controversy, but nevertheless one must not shirk an attempt at clarification. It is true that notions such as that of an ego-libido, an energy of the ego-instincts, and so on, are neither particularly easy to grasp, nor sufficiently rich in content; a speculative theory of the relations in question would begin by seeking to obtain a sharply defined concept as its basis. But I am of opinion that that is just the difference between a speculative theory and a science erected on empirical interpretation. The latter will not envy speculation its privilege of having a smooth, logically unassailable foundation, but will gladly content itself with nebulous, scarcely imaginable basic concepts, which it hopes to apprehend more clearly in the course of its development, or which it is even prepared to replace by others. For these ideas are not the foundation of science, upon which everything rests: that foundation is observation alone. They are not the bottom but the top of the whole structure, and they can be replaced and discarded without damaging it. The same thing is happening in our day in the science of physics, the basic notions of which as regards matter, centres of force, attraction, etc., are scarcely less debatable than the corresponding notions in psycho-analysis.

The value of the concepts 'ego-libido' and 'object-libido' lies in the fact that they are derived from the study of the intimate characteristics of neurotic and psychotic processes. A differentiation of libido into a kind which is proper to the ego and one which is attached to objects is an unavoidable corollary to an original hypothesis which distinguished between sexual instincts and ego-instincts. At any rate, analysis of the pure transference neuroses (hysteria and obsessional neurosis) compelled me to make this distinction and I only know that all attempts to account for these phenomena by other means have been completely unsuccessful.

In the total absence of any theory of the instincts which would help us to find our bearings, we may be permitted, or rather, it is incumbent upon us, to start off by working out some hypothesis to its logical conclusion, until it either breaks down or is confirmed. There are various points in favour of the hypothesis of there having been from the first a separation between sexual instincts and others, ego-instincts, besides the serviceability of such a hypothesis in the analysis of the transference neuroses. I admit that this latter consideration alone would not be unambiguous, for it might be a question of an indifferent psychical energy which only becomes libido through the act of cathecting an object. But, in the first place, the distinction made in this concept corresponds to the common, popular distinction between hunger and love. In the second place, there are biological considerations in its favour. The individual does actually carry on a twofold existence: one to serve his own purposes and the other as a link in a chain, which he serves against his will, or at least involuntarily. The individual himself regards sexuality as one of his own ends; whereas from another point of view he is an appendage to his germ plasm, at whose disposal he puts his energies in return for a bonus of pleasure. He is the mortal vehicle of a (possibly) immortal substance - like the inheritor of an entailed property, who is only the temporary holder of an estate which survives him. The separation of the sexual instincts from the ego-instincts would simply reflect this twofold function of the individual. Thirdly, we must recollect that all our provisional ideas in psychology will presumably some day be based on an organic substructure. This makes it probable that it is special substances and chemical processes which perform the operations of sexuality and provide for the extension of individual life into that of the species. We are taking this probability into account in replacing the special chemical substances by special psychical forces.

I try in general to keep psychology clear from everything that is different in nature from it, even biological lines of thought. For that very reason I should like at this point expressly to admit that the hypothesis of separate ego-instincts and sexual instincts (that is to say, the libido theory) rests scarcely at all upon a psychological basis, but derives its principal support from biology. But I shall be consistent enough to drop this hypothesis if psycho-analytic work should itself produce some other, more serviceable hypothesis about the instincts. So far, this has not happened. It may turn out that, most basically and on the longest view, sexual energy - libido - is only the product of a differentiation in the energy at work generally in the mind. But such an assertion has no relevance. It relates to matters which are so remote from the problems of our observation, and of which we have so little cognizance, that it is as idle to dispute it as to affirm it; this primal identity may well have as little to do with our analytic interests as the primal kinship of all the races of mankind has to do with the proof of kinship required in order to establish a legal right of inheritance. All these speculations take us nowhere. Since we cannot wait for another science to present us with the final conclusions on the theory of the instincts, it is far more to the purpose that we should try to see what light may be thrown upon this basic problem of biology by a synthesis of the *psychological* phenomena. Let us face the possibility of error; but do not let us be deterred from pursuing the logical implications of the hypothesis we first adopted of an antithesis between ego-instincts and sexual instincts (a hypothesis to which we were forcibly led by analysis of the transference neuroses), and from seeing whether it turns out to be without contradictions and fruitful, and whether it can be applied to other disorders as well, such as schizophrenia.

It would, of course, be a different matter if it were proved that the libido theory has already come to grief in the attempt to explain the latter disease. This has been asserted by C. G. Jung (1912) and it is on that account that I have been obliged to enter upon this last discussion, which I would gladly have been spared. I should have preferred to follow to its end the course embarked upon in the analysis of the Schreber case without any discussion of its premisses.

But Jung's assertion is, to say the least of it, premature. The grounds he gives for it are scanty. In the first place, he appeals to an admission of my own that I myself have been obliged, owing to the difficulties of the Schreber analysis, to extend the concept of libido (that is, to give up its sexual content) and to identify libido with psychical interest in general. Ferenczi (1913*b*), in an exhaustive criticism of Jung's work, has already said all that is necessary in correction of this erroneous interpretation. I can only corroborate his criticism and repeat that I have never made any such retractation of the libido theory. Another argument of Jung's, namely, that we cannot suppose that the withdrawal of the libido is in itself enough to bring about the loss of the normal function of reality, is no argument but a dictum. It 'begs the question',[1] and saves discussion; for whether and how this is possible was precisely the point that should have been under investigation. In his next major work, Jung (1913) just misses the solution I had long since indicated: 'At the same time', he writes, 'there is this to be further taken into consideration (a point to which, incidentally, Freud refers in his work on the Schreber case) - that the introversion of the *libido sexualis* leads to a cathexis of the "ego", and that it may possibly be this that produces the result of a loss of reality. It is indeed a tempting possibility to explain the psychology of the loss of reality in this fashion.' But Jung does not enter much further into a discussion of this possibility. A few lines later he dismisses it with the remark that this determinant 'would result in the psychology of an ascetic anchorite, not in a dementia praecox'. How little this inapt analogy can help us to decide the question may be learnt from the consideration that an anchorite of this kind, who 'tries to eradicate every trace of sexual interest' (but only in the popular sense of the word 'sexual'), does not even necessarily display any pathogenic allocation of the libido. He may have diverted his sexual interest from human beings entirely, and yet may have sublimated it into a heightened interest in the divine, in nature, or in the animal kingdom, without his libido having undergone an introversion on to his phantasies or a return to his ego. This analogy would seem to rule out in advance the possibility of differentiating between interest emanating from erotic sources and from others. Let us remember, further, that the researches of the Swiss school, however valuable, have elucidated only two features in the picture of dementia praecox - the presence in it of complexes known to us both in healthy and neurotic subjects, and the similarity of the phantasies that occur in it to popular myths - but that they have not been able to throw any further light on the mechanism of the disease. We may repudiate Jung's assertion, then, that the libido theory has come to grief in the attempt to explain dementia praecox, and that it is therefore disposed of for the other neuroses as well.

II

Certain special difficulties seem to me to lie in the way of a direct study of narcissism. Our chief means of access to it will probably remain the analysis of the paraphrenias. Just as the transference neuroses have enabled us to trace the libidinal instinctual impulses, so dementia praecox and paranoia will give us an insight into the psychology of the ego. Once more, in order to arrive at an understanding of what seems so simple in normal phenomena, we shall have to turn to the field of pathology with its distortions and exaggerations. At the same time, other means of approach remain open to us, by which we may obtain a better knowledge of narcissism. These I shall now discuss in the following order: the study of organic disease, of hypochondria and of the erotic life of the sexes.

In estimating the influence of organic disease upon the distribution of libido, I follow a suggestion made to me orally by Sándor Ferenczi. It is universally known, and we take it as a matter of course, that a person who is tormented by organic pain and discomfort gives up his interest in the things of the external world, in so far as they do not concern his suffering. Closer observation teaches us that he also

15

withdraws *libidinal* interest from his love-objects: so long as he suffers, he ceases to love. The commonplace nature of this fact is no reason why we should be deterred from translating it into terms of the libido theory. We should then say:(the sick man withdraws his libidinal cathexes back upon his own ego, and sends them out again when he recovers. 'Concentrated is his soul', says Wilhelm Busch of the poet suffering from toothache, 'in his molar's narrow hole.' Here libido and ego-interest share the same fate and are once more indistinguishable from each other. The familiar egoism of the sick person covers both. We find it so natural because we are certain that in the same situation we should behave in just the same way. The way in which a lover's feelings, however strong, are banished by bodily ailments, and suddenly replaced by complete indifference, is a theme which has been exploited by comic writers to an appropriate extent.

The condition of sleep, too, resembles illness in implying a narcissistic withdrawal of the positions of the libido on to the subject's own self, or, more precisely, on to the single wish to sleep. The egoism of dreams fits very well into this context. In both states we have, if nothing else, examples of changes in the distribution of libido that are consequent upon an alteration of the ego.

Hypochondria, like organic disease, manifests itself in distressing and painful bodily sensations, and it has the

16

same effect as organic disease on the distribution of libido. The hypochondriac withdraws both interest and libido - the latter specially markedly - from the objects of the external world and concentrates both of them upon the organ that is engaging his attention. A difference between hypochondria and organic disease now becomes evident: in the latter, the distressing sensations are based upon demonstrable changes; in the former, this is not so. But it would be entirely in keeping with our general conception of the processes of neurosis if we decided to say that hypochondria must be right: organic changes must be supposed to be present in it, too.

But what could these changes be? We will let ourselves be guided at this point by our experience, which shows that bodily sensations of an unpleasurable nature, comparable to those of hypochondria, occur in the other neuroses as well. I have said before that I am inclined to class hypochondria with neurasthenia and anxiety-neurosis as a third 'actual' neurosis. It would probably not be going too far to suppose that in the case of the other neuroses a small amount of hypochondria was regularly formed at the same time as well. We have the best example of this, I think, in anxiety neurosis with its superstructure of hysteria. Now the familiar prototype of an organ that is painfully tender, that is in some way changed and that is yet not diseased in the ordinary sense, is the genital organ in its states of excitation. In that condition it becomes congested with blood, swollen and humected, and is the seat of a multiplicity of sensations. Let us now, taking any part of the body, describe its activity of sending sexually exciting stimuli to the mind as its 'erotogenicity', and let us further reflect that the considerations on which our theory of sexuality was based have long accustomed us to the notion that certain other parts of the body - the 'erotogenic' zones - may act as substitutes for the genitals and behave analogously to them. We have then only one more step to take. We can decide to regard erotogenicity as a general characteristic of all organs and may then speak of an increase or decrease of it in a particular part of the body. For every such change in the erotogenicity of the organs there might then be a parallel change of libidinal cathexis in the ego. Such factors would constitute what we believe to underlie hypochondria and what may have the same effect upon the distribution of libido as is produced by a material illness of the organs.

We see that, if we follow up this line of thought, we come up against the problem not only of hypochondria, but of the other 'actual' neuroses - neurasthenia and anxiety neurosis. Let us therefore stop at this point. It is not within the scope of a purely psychological inquiry to penetrate so far behind the frontiers of physiological research. I will merely mention that from this point of view we may suspect that the relation of hypochondria to paraphrenia is similar to that of the other 'actual' neuroses to hysteria and obsessional neurosis: we may suspect, that is, that it is dependent on ego-libido just as the others are on object-libido, and that hypochondriacal anxiety is the counterpart, as coming from ego-libido, to neurotic anxiety. Further, since we are already familiar with the idea that the mechanism of falling ill and of the formation of symptoms in the transference neuroses - the path from introversion to regression - is to be linked to a damming-up of object-libido,[1] we may come to closer quarters with the idea of a damming-up of ego-libido as well and may bring this idea into relation with the phenomena of hypochondria and paraphrenia.

At this point, our curiosity will of course raise the question why this damming-up of libido in the ego should have to be experienced as unpleasurable. I shall content myself with the answer that unpleasure is always the expression of a higher degree of tension, and that therefore what is happening is that a quantity in the field of material events is being transformed here as elsewhere into the psychical quality of unpleasure. Nevertheless it may be that what is decisive for the generation of unpleasure is not the absolute magnitude of the material event, but rather some particular function of that absolute magnitude. Here we may even venture to touch on the question of what makes it necessary at all for our mental life to pass beyond the limits of narcissism and to attach the libido to objects. The answer which would follow from our line of thought would once more be that this necessity arises when the cathexis of the ego with libido exceeds a certain amount. A strong egoism is a protection against falling ill, but in the last resort we must begin to love in order not to fall ill, and we are bound to fall ill if, in consequence of frustration, we are unable to love. This follows somewhat on the lines of Heine's picture of the psychogenesis of the Creation:

Krankheit ist wohl der letzte Grund
Des ganzen Schöpferdrangs gewesen;
Erschaffend konnte ich genesen,
Erschaffend wurde ich gesund.[2]

We have recognized our mental apparatus as being first and foremost a device designed for mastering excitations which would otherwise be felt as distressing or would have pathogenic effects. Working them over in the mind helps remarkably towards an internal draining away of excitations which are incapable of direct discharge outwards, or for which such a discharge is for the moment undesirable. In the first instance, however, it is a matter of indifference whether this internal process of working-over is carried out upon real or imaginary objects. The difference does not appear till later - if the turning of the libido on to unreal objects (introversion) has led to its being dammed up. In paraphrenics, megalomania allows of a similar internal working-over of libido which has returned to the ego; perhaps it is only when the megalomania fails that the damming-up of libido in the ego becomes pathogenic and starts the process of recovery which gives us the impression of being a disease.

¹ Cf. 'Types of Onset of Neurosis' (1912*c*).

² ['Illness was no doubt the final cause of the whole urge to create. By creating, I could recover; by creating, I became healthy.']

I shall try here to penetrate a little further into the mechanism of paraphrenia and shall bring together those views which already seem to me to deserve consideration. The difference between paraphrenic affections and the transference neuroses appears to me to lie in the circumstance that, in the former, the libido that is liberated by frustration does not remain attached to objects in phantasy, but withdraws on to the ego. Megalomania would accordingly correspond to the psychical mastering of this latter amount of libido, and would thus be the counterpart of the introversion on to phantasies that is found in the transference neuroses; a failure of this psychical function gives rise to the hypochondria of paraphrenia and this is homologous to the anxiety of the transference neuroses. We know that this anxiety can be resolved by further psychical working over, i.e. by conversion, reaction-formation or the construction of protections (phobias). The corresponding process in paraphrenics is an attempt at restoration, to which the striking manifestations of the disease are due. Since paraphrenia frequently, if not usually, brings about only a *partial* detachment of the libido from objects, we can distinguish three groups of phenomena in the clinical picture: (1) those representing what remains of a normal state or of neurosis (residual phenomena); (2) those representing the morbid process (detachment of libido from its objects and, further, megalomania, hypochondria, affective disturbance and every kind of regression); (3) those representing restoration, in which the libido is once more attached to objects, after the manner of a hysteria (in dementia praecox or paraphrenia proper), or of an obsessional neurosis (in paranoia). This fresh libidinal cathexis differs from the primary one in that it starts from another level and under other conditions. The difference between the transference neuroses brought about in the case of this fresh kind of libidinal cathexis and the corresponding formations where the ego is normal should be able to afford us the deepest insight into the structure of our mental apparatus.

A third way in which we may approach the study of narcissism is by observing the erotic life of human beings, with its many kinds of differentiation in man and woman. Just as object-libido at first concealed ego-libido from our observation, so too in connection with the object-choice of infants (and of growing children) what we first noticed was

that they derived their sexual objects from their experiences
of satisfaction. The first auto-erotic sexual satisfactions are
experienced in connection with vital functions which serve
the purpose of self-preservation. The sexual instincts are at
the outset attached to the satisfaction of the ego-instincts;
only later do they become independent of these, and even
then we have an indication of that original attachment in
the fact that the persons who are concerned with a child's
feeding, care, and protection become his earliest sexual
objects: that is to say, in the first instance his mother or a
substitute for her. Side by side, however, with this type and
source of object-choice, which may be called the 'anaclitic'
or 'attachment' type, psycho-analytic research has revealed
a second type, which we were not prepared for finding. We
have discovered, especially clearly in people whose libidinal
development has suffered some disturbance, such as perverts
and homosexuals, that in their later choice of love-objects
they have taken as a model not their mother but their own
selves. They are plainly seeking *themselves* as a love-object,
and are exhibiting a type of object-choice which must be
termed 'narcissistic'. In this observation we have the strongest
of the reasons which have led us to adopt the hypothesis of
narcissism.

We have, however, not concluded that human beings
are divided into two sharply differentiated groups, according
as their object-choice conforms to the anaclitic or to the

narcissistic type; we assume rather that both kinds of object-choice are open to each individual, though he may show a preference for one or the other. We say that a human being has originally two sexual objects - himself and the woman who nurses him - and in doing so we are postulating a primary narcissism in everyone, which may in some cases manifest itself in a dominating fashion in his object-choice.

A comparison of the male and female sexes then shows that there are fundamental differences between them in respect of their type of object-choice, although these differences are of course not universal. Complete object-love of the attachment type is, properly speaking, characteristic of the male. It displays the marked sexual overvaluation which is doubtless derived from the child's original narcissism and thus corresponds to a transference of that narcissism to the sexual object. This sexual overvaluation is the origin of the peculiar state of being in love, a state suggestive of a neurotic compulsion, which is thus traceable to an impoverishment of the ego as regards libido in favour of the love-object. A different course is followed in the type of female most frequently met with, which is probably the purest and truest one. With the onset of puberty the maturing of the female sexual organs, which up till then have been in a condition of latency, seems to bring about an intensification of the original narcissism, and this is unfavourable to the development of a true object-choice with its accompanying sexual overvaluation. Women, especially if they grow up with good looks, develop a certain self-contentment which compensates them for the social restrictions that are imposed upon them in their choice of object. Strictly speaking, it is only themselves that such women love with an intensity comparable to that of the man's love for them. Nor does their need lie in the direction of loving, but of being loved; and the man who fulfils this condition is the one who finds favour with them. The importance of this type of woman for the erotic life of mankind is to be rated very high. Such women have the greatest fascination for men, not only for aesthetic reasons, since as a rule they are the most beautiful, but also because of a combination of interesting psychological factors. For it seems very evident that another person's narcissism has a great attraction for those who have renounced part of their own narcissism and are in search of object-love. The charm of a child lies to a great extent in his narcissism, his self-contentment and inaccessibility, just as does the charm of certain animals which seem not to concern themselves about us, such as cats and the large beasts of prey. Indeed, even great criminals and humorists, as they are represented in literature, compel our interest by the narcissistic consistency with which they manage to keep away from their ego anything that would diminish it. It is as if we envied them for maintaining a blissful state of mind - an unassailable libidinal position which we ourselves have since abandoned. The great charm of narcissistic women has, however, its reverse side; a large part of the lover's dissatisfaction, of his doubts of the woman's love, of his complaints of her enigmatic nature, has its root in this incongruity between the types of object-choice.

Perhaps it is not out of place here to give an assurance that this description of the feminine form of erotic life is not due to my tendentious desire on my part to depreciate women. Apart from the fact that tendentiousness is quite alien to me, I know that these different lines of development correspond to the differentiation of functions in a highly complicated biological whole; further, I am ready to admit that there are quite a number of women who love according to the masculine type and who also develop the sexual overvaluation proper to that type.

Even for narcissistic women, whose attitude towards men remains cool, there is a road which leads to complete object-love. In the child which they bear, a part of their own body confronts them like an extraneous object, to which, starting out from their narcissism, they can then give complete object-love. There are other women, again, who do not have to wait for a child in order to take the step in development from (secondary) narcissism to object-love. Before puberty they feel masculine and develop some way along masculine lines; after this trend has been cut short on their reaching female maturity, they still retain the capacity of longing for a masculine ideal - an ideal which is in fact a survival of the boyish nature that they themselves once possessed.

What I have so far said by way of indication may be concluded by a short summary of the paths leading to the choice of an object.

A person may love:-

(1) According to the narcissistic type:

(*a*) what he himself is (i.e. himself),

(*b*) what he himself was,

(*c*) what he himself would like to be,

(*d*) someone who was once part of himself.

(2) According to the anaclitic (attachment) type:

(*a*) the woman who feeds him,

(*b*) the man who protects him,

and the succession of substitutes who take their place. The inclusion of case (*c*) of the first type cannot be justified till a later stage of this discussion.

The significance of narcissistic object-choice for homosexuality in men must be considered in another connection.

The primary narcissism of children which we have assumed and which forms one of the postulates of our theories of the libido, is less easy to grasp by direct observation than to confirm by inference from elsewhere. If we look at the attitude of affectionate parents towards their children, we have to recognize that it is a revival and reproduction of their own narcissism, which they have long since abandoned. The trustworthy pointer constituted by overvaluation, which we have already recognized as a narcissistic stigma in the case of object-choice, dominates, as we all know, their emotional attitude. Thus they are under a compulsion to ascribe every perfection to the child - which sober observation would find no occasion to do - and to conceal and forget all his shortcomings. (Incidentally, the denial of sexuality in children is connected with this.) Moreover, they are inclined to suspend in the child's favour the operation of all the cultural acquisitions which their own narcissism has been forced to respect, and to renew on his behalf the claims to privileges which were long ago given up by themselves. The child shall have a better time than his parents; he shall not be subject to the necessities which they have recognized as paramount in life. Illness, death, renunciation of enjoyment, restrictions on his own will, shall not touch him; the laws of nature and of society shall be abrogated in his favour; he shall once more really be the centre and core of creation - 'His Majesty the Baby',[1] as we once fancied ourselves. The child shall fulfil those wishful dreams of the parents which they never carried out - the boy shall become a great man and a hero in his father's place, and the girl shall marry a prince as a tardy compensation for her mother. At the most touchy point in the narcissistic system, the immortality of the ego, which is so hard pressed by reality, security is achieved by taking refuge in the child. Parental love, which is so moving and at bottom so childish, is nothing but the parents' narcissism born again, which, transformed into object-love, unmistakably reveals its former nature.

[1] [In English in the original.]

III

The disturbances to which a child's original narcissism is exposed, the reactions with which he seeks to protect himself from them and the paths into which he is forced in doing so - these are themes which I propose to leave on one side, as an important field of work which still awaits exploration. The most significant portion of it, however, can be singled out in the shape of the 'castration complex' (in boys, anxiety about the penis - in girls, envy for the penis) and treated in connection with the effect of early deterrence from sexual activity. Psycho-analytic research ordinarily enables us to trace the vicissitudes undergone by the libidinal instincts when these, isolated from the ego-instincts, are placed in opposition to them; but in the particular field of the castration complex, it allows us to infer the existence of an epoch and a psychical situation in which the two groups of instincts, still operating in unison and inseparably mingled,

29

make their appearance as narcissistic interests. It is from this context that Adler has derived his concept of the 'masculine protest', which he has elevated almost to the position of the sole motive force in the formation of character and neurosis alike and which he bases not on a narcissistic, and therefore still a libidinal, trend, but on a social valuation. Psycho-analytic research has from the very beginning recognized the existence and importance of the 'masculine protest', but it has regarded it, in opposition to Adler, as narcissistic in nature and derived from the castration complex. The 'masculine protest' is concerned in the formation of character, into the genesis of which it enters along with many other factors, but it is completely unsuited for explaining the problems of the neuroses, with regard to which Adler takes account of nothing but the manner in which they serve the ego-instincts. I find it quite impossible to place the genesis of neurosis upon the narrow basis of the castration complex, however powerfully it may come to the fore in men among their resistances to the cure of a neurosis. Incidentally, I know of cases of neurosis in which the 'masculine protest', or, as we regard it, the castration complex, plays no pathogenic part, and even fails to appear at all.

Observation of normal adults shows that their former megalomania has been damped down and that the psychical characteristics from which we inferred their infantile narcissism have been effaced. What has become of their ego-Iibido? Are we to suppose that the whole amount of it has passed into object-cathexes? Such a possibility is plainly contrary to the whole trend of our argument; but we may find a hint at another answer to the question in the psychology of repression.

We have learnt that libidinal instinctual impulses undergo the vicissitude of pathogenic repression if they come into conflict with the subject's cultural and ethical ideas. By this we never mean that the individual in question has a merely intellectual knowledge of the existence of such ideas; we always mean that he recognizes them as a standard for himself and submits to the claims they make on him. Repression, we have said, proceeds from the ego; we might say with greater precision that it proceeds from the self-respect of the ego. The same impressions, experiences, impulses and desires that one man indulges or at least works over consciously will be rejected with the utmost indignation by another, or even stifled before they enter consciousness. The difference between the two, which contains the conditioning factor of repression, can easily be expressed in terms which enable it to be explained by the libido theory. We can say that the one man has set up an *ideal* in himself by which he measures his actual ego, while the other has formed no such ideal. For the ego the formation of an ideal would be the conditioning factor of repression.

This ideal ego is now the target of the self-love which was enjoyed in childhood by the actual ego. The subject's narcissism makes its appearance displaced on to this new ideal ego, which, like the infantile ego, finds itself possessed of every perfection that is of value. As always where the libido is concerned, man has here again shown himself incapable of giving up a satisfaction he had once enjoyed. He is not willing to forgo the narcissistic perfection of his childhood; and when, as he grows up, he is disturbed by the admonitions of others and by the awakening of his own critical judgement, so that he can no longer retain that perfection, he seeks to recover it in the new form of an ego ideal. What he projects before him as his ideal is the substitute for the lost narcissism of his childhood in which he was his own ideal.

We are naturally led to examine the relation between this forming of an ideal and sublimation. Sublimation is a process that concerns object-libido and consists in the instinct's directing itself towards an aim other than, and remote from, that of sexual satisfaction; in this process the accent falls upon deflection from sexuality. Idealization is a process that concerns the *object*; by it that object, without any alteration in its nature, is aggrandized and exalted in the subject's mind. Idealization is possible in the sphere of ego-libido as well as in that of object-libido. For example, the sexual overvaluation of an object is an idealization of it. In so far as sublimation describes something that has to do with the instinct and idealization something to do with the object, the two concepts are to be distinguished from each other.

The formation of an ego ideal is often confused with the sublimation of instinct, to the detriment of our understanding of the facts. A man who has exchanged his narcissism for homage to a high ego ideal has not necessarily on that account succeeded in sublimating his libidinal instincts. It is true that the ego ideal demands such sublimation, but it cannot enforce it; sublimation remains a special process which may be prompted by the ideal but the execution of which is entirely independent of any such prompting. It is precisely in neurotics that we find the highest differences of potential between the development of their ego ideal and the amount of sublimation of their primitive libidinal instincts; and in general it is far harder to convince an idealist of the inexpedient location of his libido than a plain man whose pretensions have remained more moderate. Further, the formation of an ego ideal and sublimation are quite differently related to the causation of neurosis. As we have learnt, the formation of an ideal heightens the demands of the ego and is the most powerful factor favouring repression; sublimation is a way out, a way by which those demands can be met *without* involving repression.

It would not surprise us if we were to find a special psychical agency which performs the task of seeing that narcissistic satisfaction from the ego ideal is ensured and which, with this end in view, constantly watches the actual ego and measures it by that ideal. If such an agency does exist, we cannot possibly come upon it as a *discovery* - we can only *recognize* it; for we may reflect that what we call our 'conscience' has the required characteristics. Recognition of this agency enables us to understand the so-called 'delusions of being noticed' or more correctly, of being *watched*, which are such striking symptoms in the paranoid diseases and which may also occur as an isolated form of illness, or intercalated in a transference neurosis. Patients of this sort complain that all their thoughts are known and their actions watched and supervised; they are informed of the functioning of this agency by voices which characteristically speak to them in the third person ('Now she's thinking of that again', 'now he's going out'). This complaint is justified; it describes the truth. A power of this kind, watching, discovering and criticizing all our intentions, does really exist. Indeed, it exists in every one of us in normal life.

Delusions of being watched present this power in a regressive form, thus revealing its genesis and the reason why the patient is in revolt against it. For what prompted the subject to form an ego ideal, on whose behalf his conscience acts as watchman, arose from the critical influence of his parents (conveyed to him by the medium of the voice), to whom were added, as time went on, those who trained and taught him and the innumerable and indefinable host of all the other people in his environment - his fellow-men - and public opinion.

In this way large amounts of libido of an essentially homosexual kind are drawn into the formation of the narcissistic ego ideal and find outlet and satisfaction in maintaining it. The institution of conscience was at bottom an embodiment, first of parental criticism, and subsequently of that of society - a process which is repeated in what takes place when a tendency towards repression develops out of a prohibition or obstacle that came in the first instance from without. The voices, as well as the undefined multitude, are brought into the foreground again by the disease, and so the evolution of conscience is reproduced regressively. But the revolt against this 'censoring agency' arises out of the subject's desire (in accordance with the fundamental character of his illness) to liberate himself from all these influences, beginning with the parental one, and out of his withdrawal of homosexual libido from them. His conscience then confronts him in a regressive form as a hostile influence from without.

The complaints made by paranoics also show that at bottom the self-criticism of conscience coincides with the self-observation on which it is based. Thus the activity of the mind which has taken over the function of conscience has also placed itself at the service of internal research, which furnishes philosophy with the material for its intellectual operations. This may have some bearing on the characteristic tendency of paranoics to construct speculative systems.[1]

> [1] I should like to add to this, merely by way of suggestion, that the developing and strengthening of this observing agency might contain within it the subsequent genesis of (subjective) memory and the time-factor, the latter of which has no application to unconscious processes.

It will certainly be of importance to us if evidence of the activity of this critically observing agency - which becomes heightened into conscience and philosophic introspection - can be found in other fields as well. I will mention here what Herbert Silberer has called the 'functional phenomenon', one of the few indisputably valuable additions to the theory of dreams. Silberer, as we know, has shown that in states between sleeping and waking we can directly observe the translation of thoughts into visual images, but that in these circumstances we frequently have a representation, not of a thought-content, but of the actual state (willingness, fatigue, etc.) of the person who is struggling against sleep. Similarly, he has shown that the conclusions of some dreams or some divisions in their content merely signify the dreamer's own perception of his sleeping and waking. Silberer has thus demonstrated the part played by observation - in the sense of the paranoic's delusions of being watched - in the formation of dreams. This part is not a constant one. Probably the reason why I overlooked it is because it does not play any great part in my own dreams; in persons who are gifted philosophically and accustomed to introspection it may become very evident.

We may here recall that we have found that the formation of dreams takes place under the dominance of a censorship which compels distortion of the dream-thoughts. We did not, however, picture this censorship as a special power, but chose the term to designate one side of the repressive trends that govern the ego, namely the side which is turned towards the dream-thoughts. If we enter further into the structure of the ego, we may recognize in the ego ideal and in the dynamic utterances of conscience the *dream-censor* as well. If this censor is to some extent on the alert even during sleep, we can understand how it is that its suggested activity of self-observation and self-criticism - with such thoughts as, 'now he is too sleepy to think', 'now he is waking up' - makes a contribution to the content of the dream.[1]

[1] I cannot here determine whether the differentiation of the censoring agency from the rest of the ego is capable of forming the basis of the philosophic distinction between consciousness and self-consciousness.

At this point we may attempt some discussion of the self-regarding attitude in normal people and in neurotics.

In the first place self-regard appears to us to be an expression of the size of the ego; what the various elements are which go to determine that size is irrelevant. Everything a person possesses or achieves, every remnant of the primitive feeling of omnipotence which his experience has confirmed, helps to increase his self-regard.

Applying our distinction between sexual and ego-instincts, we must recognize that self-regard has a specially intimate dependence on narcissistic libido. Here we are supported by two fundamental facts: that in paraphrenics self-regard is increased, while in the transference neuroses it is diminished; and that in love-relations not being loved lowers the self-regarding feelings, while being loved raises them. As we have indicated, the aim and the satisfaction in a narcissistic object-choice is to be loved.

Further, it is easy to observe that libidinal object-cathexis does not raise self-regard. The effect of dependence upon the loved object is to lower that feeling: a person in love is humble. A person who loves has, so to speak, forfeited a part of his narcissism, and it can only be replaced by his being loved. In all these respects self-regard seems to remain related to the narcissistic element in love.

The realization of impotence, of one's own inability to love, in consequence of mental or physical disorder, has an exceedingly lowering effect upon self-regard. Here, in my judgement, we must look for one of the sources of the feelings of inferiority which are experienced by patients suffering from the transference neuroses and which they are so ready to report. The main source of these feelings is, however, the impoverishment of the ego, due to the extraordinarily large libidinal cathexes which have been withdrawn from it - due, that is to say, to the injury sustained by the ego through sexual trends which are no longer subject to control.

Adler is right in maintaining that when a person with an active mental life recognizes an inferiority in one of his organs, it acts as a spur and calls out a higher level of performance in him through overcompensation. But it would be altogether an exaggeration if, following Adler's example, we sought to attribute every successful achievement to this factor of an original inferiority of an organ. Not all artists are handicapped with bad eyesight, nor were all orators originally stammerers. And there are plenty of instances of excellent achievements springing from *superior* organic endowment. In the aetiology of neuroses organic inferiority and imperfect development play an insignificant part - much the same as that played by currently active perceptual material in the formation of dreams. Neuroses make use of such inferiorities as a pretext, just as they do of every other suitable factor. We may be tempted to believe a neurotic woman patient when she tells us that it was inevitable she should fall ill, since she is ugly, deformed or lacking in charm, so that no one could love her; but the very next neurotic will teach us better - for she persists in her neurosis and in her aversion to sexuality, although she seems more desirable, and is more desired, than the average woman. The majority of hysterical women are among the attractive and even beautiful representatives of their sex, while, on the other hand, the frequency of ugliness, organic defects and infirmities in the lower classes of society does not increase the incidence of neurotic illness among them.

The relations of self-regard to erotism - that is, to libidinal object-cathexes - may be expressed concisely in the following way. Two cases must be distinguished, according to whether the erotic cathexes are ego-syntonic, or, on the contrary, have suffered repression. In the former case (where the use made of the libido is ego-syntonic), love is assessed like any other activity of the ego. Loving in itself, in so far as it involves longing and deprivation, lowers self-regard; whereas being loved, having one's love returned, and possessing the loved object, raises it once more. When libido is repressed, the erotic cathexis is felt as a severe depletion of the ego, the satisfaction of love is impossible, and the re-enrichment of the ego can be effected only by a withdrawal of libido from its objects. The return of the object-libido to the ego and its transformation into narcissism represents, as it were, a happy love once more; and, on the other hand, it is also true that a real happy love corresponds to the primal condition in which object-libido and ego-libido cannot be distinguished.

The importance and extensiveness of the topic must be my justification for adding a few more remarks which are somewhat loosely strung together.

The development of the ego consists in a departure from primary narcissism and gives rise to a vigorous attempt to recover that state. This departure is brought about by means of the displacement of libido on to an ego ideal imposed from without; and satisfaction is brought about from fulfilling this ideal.

At the same time the ego has sent out the libidinal object-cathexes. It becomes impoverished in favour of these cathexes, just as it does in favour of the ego ideal, and it enriches itself once more from its satisfactions in respect of the object, just as it does by fulfilling its ideal.

One part of self-regard is primary - the residue of infantile narcissism; another part arises out of the omnipotence which is corroborated by experience (the fulfilment of the ego ideal), whilst a third part proceeds from the satisfaction of object-libido.

The ego ideal has imposed severe conditions upon the satisfaction of libido through objects; for it causes some of them to be rejected by means of its censor, as being incompatible. Where no such ideal has been formed, the sexual trend in question makes its appearance unchanged in the personality in the form of a perversion. To be their own ideal once more, in regard to sexual no less than other

41

trends, as they were in childhood - this is what people strive to attain as their happiness.

Being in love consists in a flowing-over of ego-libido on to the object. It has the power to remove repressions and re-instate perversions. It exalts the sexual object into a sexual ideal. Since, with the object type (or attachment type), being in love occurs in virtue of the fulfilment of infantile conditions for loving, we may say that whatever fulfils that condition is idealized.

The sexual ideal may enter into an interesting auxiliary relation to the ego ideal. It may be used for substitutive satisfaction where narcissistic satisfaction encounters real hindrances. In that case a person will love in conformity with the narcissistic type of object-choice, will love what he once was and no longer is, or else what possesses the excellences which he never had at all (cf. (c)). The formula parallel to the one there stated runs thus: what possesses the excellence which the ego lacks for making it an ideal, is loved. This expedient is of special importance for the neurotic, who, on account of his excessive object-cathexes, is impoverished in his ego and is incapable of fulfilling his ego ideal. He then seeks a way back to narcissism from his prodigal expenditure of libido upon objects, by choosing a sexual ideal after the narcissistic type which possesses the excellences to which he cannot attain. This is the cure by love, which he generally prefers to cure by analysis. Indeed, he cannot believe in any other mechanism of cure; he usually brings expectations of this sort with him to the treatment and directs them towards the person of the physician. The patient's incapacity for love, resulting from his extensive repressions, naturally stands in the way of a therapeutic plan of this kind. An unintended result is often met with when, by means of the treatment, he has been partially freed from his repressions: he withdraws from further treatment in order to choose a love-object, leaving his cure to be continued by a life with someone he loves. We might be satisfied with this result, if it did not bring with it all the dangers of a crippling dependence upon his helper in need.

The ego ideal opens up an important avenue for the understanding of group psychology. In addition to its individual side, this ideal has a social side; it is also the common ideal of a family, a class or a nation. It binds not only a person's narcissistic libido, but also a considerable amount of his homosexual libido, which is in this way turned back into the ego. The want of satisfaction which arises from the non-fulfilment of this ideal liberates homosexual libido, and this is transformed into a sense of guilt (social anxiety). Originally this sense of guilt was a fear of punishment by the parents, or, more correctly, the fear of losing their love; later the parents are replaced by an indefinite number of fellow-men. The frequent causation of paranoia by an injury to the ego, by a frustration of satisfaction within the sphere of the ego ideal, is thus made more intelligible, as is the convergence of ideal-formation and sublimation in the ego ideal, as well as the involution of sublimations and the possible transformation of ideals in paraphrenic disorders.

37241031R00031

Made in the USA
Middletown, DE
23 February 2019